Love Your Guinea Pig

Love Your Guinea Pig

by Chris Henwood

W. Foulsham & Co. Ltd.
London · New York · Toronto · Cape Town · Sydney

Acknowledgements

I would like to extend my thanks to a number of people who have helped me with my knowledge of guinea pigs over the years, and with stock including; Cath Whiteway, Prof C Keeling, Sue Pearce, Clare Hodges and The Bartlett Family

Photographs
Mike Roles Studio

Page 2: Rex Coated Tort and White female with Golden and White male

W. Foulsham & Company Limited
Yeovil Road, Slough, Berkshire, SL1 4JH

ISBN 0-572-01307-8

Photoset in Great Britain by
Dialogue 37-42 Compton Street, London EC1 V OAP
and printed in Spain by Cayfosa. Barcelona
De. Leg. B-33253-1985

Contents

Introduction

The Guinea Pig, or, to give it its proper name, the Cavy is one of the oldest and most widely kept of all small pets. Its popularity is well founded. Guinea Pigs are chunky animals with a sociable, yet rather timid nature. They are unable to jump or climb and are less likely to gnaw at their hutches than most other rodents. They may be kept in pairs or in family groups. They don't breed as often as other small rodents and their litters are relatively small.

Guinea Pigs have been retained as pets in Europe for more than four hundred years. They arrived here after the conquest of the South American Empire of the Incas by the Spanish.

Where the name Guinea Pig originated from is not known as this rodent is neither related to the Pig nor is it from Guinea. It is true however, that the ships carrying the guinea pigs from South America often arrived in Europe via the coast of Guinea and this may well have led people to believe that they actually come from there rather than South America. Another, and probably more correct suggestion is that since many individuals were exported from Guiana in northern South America, people confused the name of Guiana with Guinea.

There are a number of different types or varieties of guinea pig: those with smooth coats; rough rosetted coats; long-haired and rex coated. These different varieties are usually referred to as pure bred and these I will deal with in more detail later. You may also see what is known as crossbred varieties, in other words animals produced as a result of mating one of the pure bred varieties to another. To my mind no variety is better to keep than any other although the long haired varieties' show coats require a lot of attention and these varieties are best left until you have some experience of others. However, if you wish to enter your guinea pig for shows you will only be able to do this if it is regarded as a *recognised breed* unless that particular show has a pets only section.

---

1 Choosing Your Guinea Pig

When buying a guinea pig of any variety, it is always wise to go to a good pet shop or a private breeder. If you intend to breed for a particular colour or variety, it is almost essential to go to a private breeder. This is not to say however that you will not be able to obtain a good *pure bred* animal from a pet shop, merely that from a private breeder you are more likely to obtain exactly what you require, when you require it.

Please do not try to look around for bargains or the cheapest animals available, good guinea pigs are not that expensive.

If you want your guinea pig as a pet rather than for show, it is best to buy it when it is between six and twelve weeks of age. Since guinea pigs are sociable by nature, it is best to retain them in pairs or colonies or even with a rabbit. Should you decide to purchase a pair and you do not wish to breed; it is best to select two females. Two adult males will usually fight unless they have been raised together and occasionally even then. If however, you still only wish to keep one individual, a bachelor guinea pig will be quite happy providing that he is given a good deal of attention, and affection.

When choosing your guinea pig, take a couple of minutes to watch it in the hutch or run. Moving slowly and smoothly and avoiding any sudden movements,

Healthy guinea pig

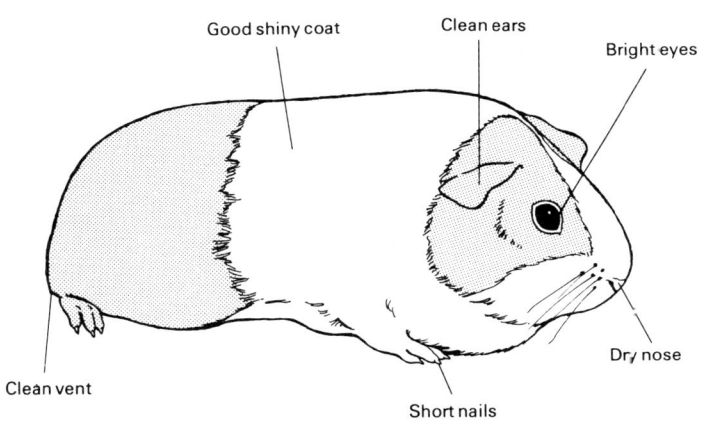

Good shiny coat

Clean ears

Bright eyes

Dry nose

Clean vent

Short nails

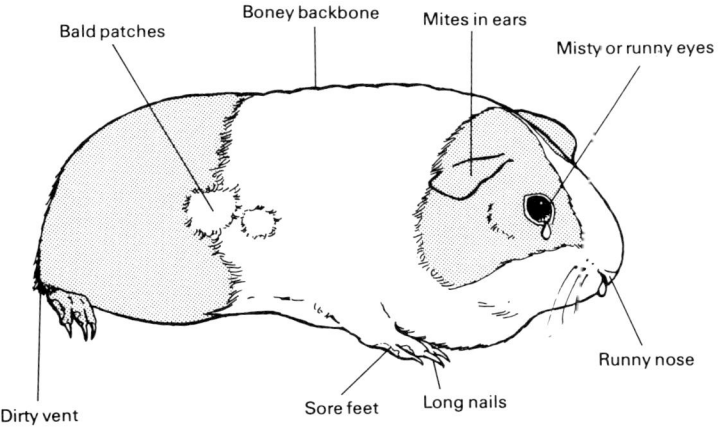

Bald patches

Boney backbone

Mites in ears

Misty or runny eyes

Dirty vent

Sore feet

Long nails

Runny nose

Unhealthy guinea pig

reach out towards your chosen animal. If it is interested and aware of your hand, although a little shy, chances are that it will tame well.

Disposition does run in varieties and some colours are much more highly strung than others.

Before actually purchasing your guinea pig, it is important to handle it. Ask the pet shop owner or the breeder to get him or her out of the cage for you. The animal should be alert with nice bright clear eyes, he should have a nice firm feel to him and should not feel skinny or thin. The nails should not be too long and the coat should be nice and thick with no bald or thin patches.

Varieties of Guinea Pigs

Today there are a great number of different varieties of Guinea Pig or Cavy available: some new, some old, some popular and some not so.

Each variety however has what is known as a standard. This is simply a description of the particular variety giving details of what an ideal animal of that particular variety should look like. I have listed a number of the various varieties and what they look like. I have not listed the exact standard word for word as this is rather boring. I hope that these outline descriptions will make you want to learn more about each variety. You can then go along to a show and ask the breeders more about the variety you have decided on.

The varieties themselves can be generally divided into two groups; the Self and the Non-Self.

The latter can be divided into a number of other smaller goups: The Smooth-Haired patterned varieties, Crested, Abyssinian, Long-Haired and Rex.

The Self Varieties

A self guinea pig is basically an animal that is the same colour all over with a smooth short-haired coat. The basic standards or requirements apply to all different colours of the Self guinea pig.

There are thirty points for colour in the self standard but there are nearly as many for *type* (twenty five). Type is best described as the shape of the guinea pig. It should have a broad head, a short face with plenty of space between the large eyes, broad high shoulders and the ears should be petal-shaped and drooping.

You can usually tell at an early age what type an adult is likely to have. But young guinea pigs are apt to be a bit long and skinny while they are growing up, so do not be disappointed if they appear not to look as good as young adults as they did as babies. The phase should not last long.

The coat should be short and silky, and grooming is important in a show animal. It should be done on a regular basis not only just before a show. Groom out the long guard hairs by drawing your thumb and forefinger along them; then rub from head to rump with your hands. A rub with a piece of silk or velvet will give them that extra shine.

Self Black

Probably the most popular of all the Self varieties. Naturally the coat is a rich deep black, common faults areared or white hairs and poor undercolour and poor type. There are many good Self Blacks about ard they very often take the Best In Show awards.

Pink- Eyed White Self

Also an extremely popular variety. For some reason they always appear to have excellent type in good show individuals. They are not plagued by hairs of the other colours nor with poor undercolour, although they maybe difficult to keep clean and do on occasions suffer from badly stained fur.

Dark- Eyed White

A recent addition to the Self group only having acquired its full standard in the last year or so. The major fault with this variety is the poor type of head in comparison with that of the Red-Eyed White. They also tend to have slight pigmentation on the feet and ears. This maybe bred out, but doing so often leads to the loss of eye pigmentation as well. This variety therefore presents a great challenge especially when you take into account the problems of stained coats as well.

Self Cream

Another variety with exceptionally good type and shape. It has dark ruby eyes that look almost black in certain lights, which set off the cream colour to perfection. The standard calls for a pale even colour with under colour to match and free from lemon or yellow tinge. However there are a number of different shades of cream throughout the country ranging from almost apricot to off white. It should actually be the colour of the cream at the top of a bottle of jersey milk. A dark Cream is too like the Buff while a lighter Cream looks like a badly stained White.

Skill in breeding is also rather necessary as litters tend to contain different shades of Cream and you cannot just breed any colour shade to any other. It is probably best to breed dark to light to maintain a fairly even colour. It is undoubtedly one of my favourites among the Selfs.

Self Golden

Another variety whose colour varies greatly, from brassy yellow to almost pale red. There are actually two varieties, as with the White; both Red-Eyed and Black-Eyed. The Red-Eyed are the better established and tend to have better type. The Dark-Eyed variety, at the time of writing, is not recognised as a full standard by the British Cavy Council. As with the White the Dark-Eyed Golden often does not have a good pigment of the ears and feet without diluting the eye colour.

Self Lilac

One of my favourites among the Self varieties, it really has to be seen to be appreciated; it can be best described as a sort of dove grey with a pinkish tinge. The young are born dark and pale as they grow. It is the pink-eyed dilute of the Black, and has a slight resemblance to the Beige. Again this variety tends to have quite good type. However over the past few years they have appeared more rarely on the show bench than they once did.

Self Chocolate

The Self Chocolate should be a rich dark chocolate (not a pale *milk* chocolate), with eyes to match. Their biggest fault is undoubtedly colour and often as not the presence of white or golden hairs particularly on the belly. The type has improved over recent years but it is still not up to the standard of the Black and Pink-Eyed White.

Self Red

A colour that appears to have rather fallen from grace over recent times. Although from speaking to various fanciers this appears to be more to lack of stock availability rather than dislike of the colour. It should be a rich dark mahogany with ears and feet to match. As with the Lilac they tend to lighten with age, therefore the best young Reds to keep are the darkest. It is also for this reason that their show life tends to be rather limited.

Self Beige

The Self Beige is actually the pink-eyed dilute of the chocolate. The best way of describing it is a very pale beige with a pink tinge. In a litter of young Beige, you will find many shades from very dark to very light. Keep the dark sows for breeding, but use a light boar or vice versa. You don't usually have to worry about the undercolour as the colour goes right down to the skin.

Non-Self Varieties

The Non-Self Varieties include Smooth Coated, Long-Haired, Rex and Rosetted. Each has its own standard as accepted and approved by its own specialist club and/or the National Cavy Club. Some are rather new to the show scene or are rather rare and these are catered for by the Rare Varieties Cavy Club.

Self Red male

The Abyssinian

This variety is usually referred to by its owners as the Abby, and is probably the most popular and well known of all the non-self varieties. This maybe because it requires much less show preparation than other varieties. It is a Rosetted, Rough Coated guinea pig often confused with the Peruvian which is in fact the long-haired mutation of the Abby. The rosettes and ridges, are formed by the unusual way in which the hair grows and these are the most important points in a show Abyssinian.

Colour is actually unimportant. An Abby maybe any colour or combination of colours. The most popular are the *mixed*, for example: Roan, Brindles and Tortoiseshell and White. Self coloured individuals, particularly Whites tend to have much softer coats and therefore lose points on the show bench.

The ideal Abby should have four rosettes in a straight line over the saddle of the body, four around the rump, and one or two on each shoulder. Where the hair growing in one direction from one rosette, meets the

Abyssinian Strawberry Roan females

hair growing in the opposite direction from another rosette, it forms a ridge. The rosettes should be so placed that the ridges run in straight lines, both across the body and down the back and sides. The rosettes themselves should be deep with hairs radiating from a pin-point centre. The coat should be harsh, and there should be no flat smooth coat anywhere and this includes the head.

The Abby has the appearance of having a Frans-Joseph moustache. There are a number of faults in the Abby, and usually you can tell these at birth. For example out of line or double centred rosettes, uneven ridges, soft or long coat, although young animals coats are often softer than they will be as adults.

Abbys are lively individuals, some are often rather nervous and boars (males) are often rather agressive towards other boars, more so than in most other varieties.

The Dutch

The Dutch guinea pig is a smooth-coated variety, it is basically a white animal with coloured markings. The commonest being the Red and the Black but it also occurs in Chocolate, Cream, Golden, Agouti and even Tri-Colour.

This is a very distinctive variety. The rear part of the body should be coloured and the front white. The demarcation is a straight line round the body as near to the front legs as possible, without the colour being present on the legs themselves. This is known as the saddle. The hind legs should have white socks of equal length going half way up to the first joint and having straight demarcation lines round the foot. These socks

Red and Chocolate Dutch

are known as stops. The markings on the face should be as round as possible, including the eyes and ears, reaching to the whiskers but not actually including them. The colour should not run onto the neck or under the chin, and the markings on either side of the face should be separated by a wedge-shaped blaze of white, extending up the centre of the face to between the ears. The markings on each side of the head and body should be identical, giving a well balanced appearance. Naturally this is the ideal and few actually achieve this. Most Dutch even on the Show bench have a few faults, the most common being cheek markings covering the whiskers; stops too short or too long or even no stops at all. Flesh coloured marks on the ears are another major problem. Ears should be coloured both inside and out. Eyes should match the coloured portions of the body.

Agouti

Agouti guinea pigs have a ticked or speckled appearance, this is caused if coloured hairs are interspersed with plain coloured hairs. The most popular colours are the Golden and Silver, but there are a few other varieties although these are not popular with most Agouiti judges.

Golden Agouti

The most commonly seen, it has a black ground colour ticked with golden and has a golden belly colour.

Silver Agouti

This is one of my personal favourite varieties. The ground colour is blue-black ticked with silver grey. The belly is a dark silvery grey.

Cinnamon Agouti

The most popular of the rarer Agoutis. The ground colour is light Chocolate ticked with silver and a dark cinnamon belly colour.

Lemon Agouti

A common Agouti colour among pet owners but rather looked down upon by the 'true' Agouti fanciers. Two varieties are possible: a Black based and a Chocolate based (also known as the Chocolate Agouti). Both have cream ticking and a creamy yellow belly colour.

Orange Agouti

A rare variety, similar to the Golden but it has Chocolate ground colour rather than the Black of the Golden.

Cinnamon Agouti male

Orange, Golden and Lemon Agouti

Rare Varieties of Agouti

It is also possible to produce Agoutis in dilute colours for example: Beige/Golden and Lilac/Cream. These are pink-eyed and are known as Argentes and are catered for by the Rare Varieties Cavy Club and will therefore be dealt with a little later.

The major faults with the Agouti guinea pigs are: long coarse guard hairs which spoil the appearance of the ticking; uneven grooming which often leaves large dark patches on the coat; eye circles (a circle of lighter coloured hair around the eyes); Feet and belly that do not match the body colour, and single rather than Agouti coloured patches.

Tortoiseshell and White

A Tort and White, as this variety is more commonly known, is a smooth, short coated guinea pig, with a patchwork colour of red, black and white. Each patch should be as square as possible with straight demarcation lines between the patches. The opposing patches on each side of the body should be of a different colour. The demarcation line between the sides should run in a straight line, from the tip of the nose, between the ears, down the centre of the rump, between the legs, down the cente of the belly and under the chin to the nose again. It is probably the most striking and beautiful of the guinea pigs and yet also the most heart breaking. The reason for this is that you may well breed more than a hundred individuals without breeding one single show standard individual, no matter how good your foundation stock. On the other hand you could obtain two almost perfect individuals in a single litter. It is because of this that you often find that the Tort and White are kept by fanciers with a lot of room for keeping them in quite large numbers. I have never retained this variety other than as a pet, but most Tort Breeders seem to agree that the major faults to avoid when buying breeding stock are:

1. Breeching; this is when one colour runs right around the rump.
2. Banding; a band of one colour going part or all the way around the body.
3. Brindling; patches of hairs of intermingled colours.

Look for breeding stock with clean cut patches of colour even if it is cut in the wrong place. A nice straight belly line, even if it is uneven on the top also appears to be very important.

Himalayan

The Himmy as it is commonly called can best be described as being similar to a Siamese cat in colour. It has a light body colour and dark points. The body should be as white as possible, and the points; the nose, ears and feet, should be as dark as possible in either of the two recognised colours, Black and Chocolate. The eyes are red.

The babies are born pure white but within a few days the pigment on the legs begins to show through, although the fur on the points is not completely dark until about 5-6 months old. The point of dark colour on the nose is usually known as the smut and this should be as large as possible extending up to the nose between the eyes and down into the whiskers. The smut is important as in judging it is worth the most points. The ears should be a matching colour and as with all varieties nicely drooping. The colour on the legs must go well up the leg but not beyond the hock.

The show life of the Himmy is rather restricted, as young ones under five months do not really have the dense points. These are usually interspersed with white hairs which gradually disappear as they grow older. Again as adults they start to lose density and the white hairs again begin to appear.

Faults to look for in young stock are white toes or toe nails, white patches on the feet and flesh coloured patches on the ears. Some also have dark rumps and these will probably retain this as adults. They will not be suitable for showing, but do not discard these individuals particularly if they are sows, as they are useful breeders. Discard only those with white feet.

Do not expect Himalayans to be big guinea pigs, they are naturally a small variety, although the Chocolates do tend to be slightly larger than the Black.

Crested Guinea Pigs

This is not a very old variety, but in its short life it has gained great ground. As a variety it originally occurred in the USA and was introduced to the UK by Isobel Turner in 1972 when she imported six individuals from Canada.

The Crest is on the head in a form of a rosette, situated centrally above the eyes but below the ears. The hairs of the crest radiate from a central point. Apart from the crest, the animal should be smooth coated. There are two basic Crested types: the English and the American. The English is a Self coloured animal with the

Self and Crested Creams

crest the same colour as that of the body.

 The American is a Self coloured animal with a crest of a contrasting colour. Probably the most popular is the White Crested Golden.

Roans and Dalmations

Although these two varieties are not related, they have a joint club and are usually classed together at shows.

Roan

The smooth Roan was developed after many years of selective breeding by Jan Belling. It is basically a black cavy with white hairs evenly intermixed throughout the body. Solid black should be confined to the head and feet, but white whiskers should not be penalised.

The eye colour is black but, in certain lights this may well appear to be ruby. This is not a fault.

Dalmation

This is a spotted variety and is accepted in any Self or Agouti colour. It actually envolved from a mutation of Self Blacks and was originally bred by Elizabeth Wilson.

The Dalmation should have black or corresponding colours, or silvered head, with a blaze, ruby eyes and coloured or silvered feet, to match the head. Faults include: the lack of a blaze, spotting too heavy, uneven or too light.

Note Some difficulties arise if Roan are bred to Roan or Dalmation to Dalmation. This usually results in about one in four of the babies being born with small, practically non existent eyes. In colour they are pure white and are known as *Micropthalmic White*. They rarely live more than a few weeks. To avoid this, breed Roans and Dalmations to the Self coloured guinea pigs which are bred from these varieties.

Peruvian

This is one of the Long-Haired members of the Guinea Pig family. More care and attention must be given to the Peruvian than any other guinea pig variety. It is a full time occupation to breed and show Peruvians. *This is not a*

Dalmatian female and young male

beginner's guinea pig. The owner must be prepared to brush and rearrange the longhair every day. Anyone contemplating this breed should join the Peruvian Cavy Club, who will give information on the do's and don'ts, which, because of lack of space, I am unable to do here.

Genetically the Peruvian is a Long-Haired Abyssian. The rosetting makes the hair on the top of the body lie towards the head and fall over the face, while the hair at the rear end falls over the hindquarters making it difficult to tell which end is which.

Not all Peruvians have the temperament to sit still on their special show stands as they are required to when being judged. The reason they have these special stands is so as not to spoil their long coats which may well grow up to 50 cms (20 inches) or more. When Peruvians are born they are short-coated and should have two rosettes sited on the rump, but the hair does not grow towards the rump but towards the ears. Only the hair below the rosettes grows downwards. As the animal ages the hair will start to part up the middle and should be encouraged downwards on each side of the parting. Eventually the hair is brushed over the two rosettes into what is called the sweep and when long enough, at about 12 weeks of age it is taken up into what is called a wrapper made of paper and a small piece of balsa wood and secured with a rubber band. At about 5½ – 6 months of age the side hair is placed into side wrappers; one on each side. This is where problems begin as these are inclined to come out rather easily, though as the hair gets longer they do stay in more easily.

If a cavy objects very strongly to having wrappers and will not sit still, you might as well give up on that particular animal. Obviously wrapping is only for show stock. Breeding stock should have their coats clipped, but care should still be taken as they do need to be brushed and bathed as the coats can quickly become matted even when clipped.

The colour of a Peruvian does not matter as it is the coat that is the most important feature.

Sheltie

The Sheltie, like the Peruvian, is a Long-Haired guinea pig and needs a lot of care and attention. The difference

Adult Coronet with brushed out show coat

between the two is that the Sheltie is the Long-Haired variety of the smooth guinea pig. The Sheltie's hair flows backwards leaving the head clear and forms a long train at the rear. Baby shelties look quite different from the powder puff baby Peruvians. They look the same as baby smooth, short-coated varieties, but their coats grow quite quickly. It is necessary to train them in the same way as the Peruvian and as with the Peruvian I would suggest that you join the Sheltie Cavy Club, which will

Adult Coronet in wrappers

help you with the do's and don'ts. Some people only put a paper wrapper in the train of a Sheltie, while others put in side wrappers as well. The Shelties should be clipped for breeding.

Coronet

The Coronet is basically a Crested Sheltie and should be treated in the same way as the Sheltie although it does have its own breed club.

Rare and New Varieties

When first formed, the Rare Varieties Cavy Club catered for only two varieties; the Tortoiseshell and Brindle. Now it has taken under its wing any new variety which is considered worthwhile. The Rare Varieties can be sub divided into the following:

1. Standardised
2. Guide Standard
3. Unstandardised

Standardised

These are in general those that have reached a standard of excellence, which the RVCC and the British Cavy Council have accepted and provided a standard for.

When breeders of a Standardised rare variety feel that they are strong enough in numbers they may form a specialist club for that variety. Before this can take place, however, they must first apply to the club which caters for them. This is usually the RVCC, and then take their proposal, through their representative to the BCC. If they accept and pass the proposal then the fanciers can go ahead and form their new club.

A variety can, in the same way be taken over by an existing club. The Dark Eyed White, was adopted by the English Self Cavy Club, but at the time of writing they have not accepted the D.E. Golden or Buff.

The Standardised Varieties are:

Tortoiseshells

Rather few and far between and although it is an old variety it has never attained popularity. The Tort, is basically similar to the Tort and White; but minus the White. They are even more difficult to breed to show standard than the Tort and White. It should have clearly defined patches of red and black.

Brindles

Again an old variety, but not popular. these should have an even intermingling of black and red hairs all over the body. It is very difficult to achieve and I feel that breeders of this variety deserve great admiration for their perseverence.

Tri-Colours and Bi-Colours

Tri-Colours are patched as Tortoiseshell and White but in different colours, for example: Chocolate/Cream/White, Golden Agouti/Golden/White.

Bi-Colours are patched as Tortoiseshells but again in different colours, for example: Black/White, Chocolate/Cream.

Rex

At the time of writing the Rex guinea pig has only just attained its full standard. The Rex is to my mind one of the most exciting of the new varieties and is increasing in numbers greatly. It is my personal favourite. The coat appears woolly, because the guard hairs of the normal coat are very much shortened. This has the effect that the coat will not lie flat but curls and stands upright. The coat should be dense and short. Any colour is permissible. Rex bred to Rex will breed true but bred to a Self you will only obtain Selfs although some will be carriers and these are useful for breeding. There's also a

Dominant Rex variety; in this case only one animal needs to be Rex to produce Rex young but these are very few in numbers.

Blacks: Self, Crested and Rex

Guide Standard

The British Cavy Council are trying to dis-continue 'Unstandardised' classes at shows, in favour of guide standard classes. In this way judges would at least have a general guide to what to look for in a new variety. However, many shows still put on unstandardised classes.

Before a Guide Standard is accepted it must be put forward by the RVCC to the BCC.

Guide Standards already accepted are:

Argente

This is really a Red-Eyed Agouti. The colour accepted by the BCC is lilac based with Golden ticking. There are other varieties for example the Beige based Argente but these have not been accepted by the BCC.

Dark-Eyed Golden

The Dark-Eyed Golden Self, apart from the Crested variety, has not yet been accepted by the BCC and the English Self Cavy Club. They should follow the pattern set for the Red-Eyed Golden, but should have dark eyes, either black or ruby.

Harlequin

This is yet another patchwork guinea pig. The patches are of two colours and a roaned or brindled mixture of the two, for example; Black, White and Blue Roan (Known as the Magpie) or Chocolate, Cream and Choc/Cream Roan. The head markings should have half of the head one colour and the other half the other colour or Roan, with a straight dividing line down the centre of the face. Feet should be alternate colours, around the body. A difficult guinea pig, to breed but becoming more popular.

Saffron

Could be described as a Red-Eyed Buff, but should be rather brighter in colour than the Buff and more lemonish.

Harlequin male

Unstandardised

These are varieties which are awaiting a guide standard, but have been approved by the RVCC.

Buffs

One of my favourite Selfs, although many people consider these as no more than dark Creams. Buff bred to Buff breed true and do not produce Cream. They are dark — eyed and can be confused with Saffron, however Saffron has red eyes.

Buff and Beige

An extremely attractive guinea pig, Chocolate on the back and shading gradually to Beige or Cream on the belly. They can be dark, medium or light coloured. They are at present extremely rare.

New Varieties

New varieties crop up from time to time. One that has appeared recently is the Satin which was imported from North America in 1982/83. The Satin has a very shiny coat. At the moment it is extremely rare but I think it will become very popular in a few years.

2 Housing

The housing of guinea pigs is relatively easy. They do not require elaborate cages, but they do need adequate protection from variable weather conditions. I would suggest that unless you can provide an extremely warm, weatherproof hutch (these are both difficult to obtain and usually expensive) you site your cages or hutches in a wooden shed or outhouse. This should have adequate ventilation. Garages should be avoided unless they are unoccupied by cars, as the car fumes are very dangerous to guinea pigs and may even kill if the fumes are allowed to gather in a garage.

The advantage of having your stock under cover is that it makes looking after them a much more comfortable task for yourself and provides protection from both draughts and damp for the guinea pigs.

Whilst guinea pigs do not need elaborate cages or hutches, they should not be shoddily built. They should be so constructed so that they give good protection from draughts. As a general rule each animal requires 1860 sq cms of floor space, and this area is also quite adequate for a sow and her litter. If your cavies are all together as a colony, they would be quite happy with a floor area of 930 sq cms each. Many breeders use large hutches 40 cms high and 50 cms deep but of great length, these are then partitioned into suitable units to provide the required floor space for each group.

Unfortunately the general pet shop hutches sold for

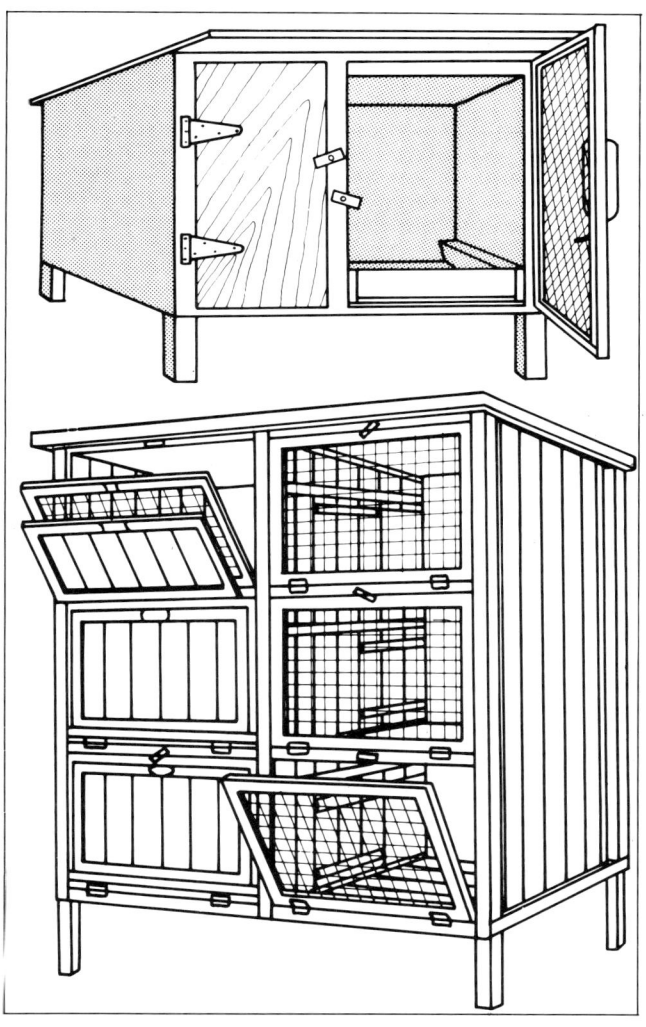

Types of hutches

guinea pigs are usually too small and often even made of metal, which is most unsuitable. They are also on the whole far too expensive for the average guinea pig owner who may well have 20 or more guinea pigs. There are however a number of companies throughout the country that manufacture hutches especially for guinea pigs and these are usually more reasonably priced, particularly if you require quite a number of hutches in order to establish a breeding stud.

However it is much cheaper to make your own cages.

Wood is the best material for hutches, but as it absorbs moisture it is quite a good idea to fit a piece of wood in the form of a tray to cover the base of the hutch. This extra piece can then be renewed when necessary Please do not use wire floors, they are not suitable for guinea pigs. Make the hutches so that the front opens completely; this makes it easier to clean out. A piece of wood about two inches high, fitted across the open front of the hutch, but removable for cleaning, ensures that your animals will not fall out when you open the hutch door. If your hutches are in a shed then the entire front may be of wire netting. No artificial heating of the shed should be necessary, but the shed should be weatherproof and draughtproof.

If you cannot manage to keep the hutches in a shed or garage or you need extra hutch space, it may well be necessary to have outdoor hutches. Naturally these should be more substantial than the indoor ones, well able to withstand all types of weather, giving the protection to the guinea pigs at all times. They should have a separate sheltered nest compartment, with an opening into the main part of the hutch to give the guinea pigs (allow room for large pregnant ones) easy access. This nest area gives the animals somewhere warm in the winter and cool in the summer. The roof and sides should be covered with roofing felt so that damp cannot get in. There should be some form of shutter that can be fixed over the wire front at night and in really bad weather. This shutter should leave about an inch of clear space at the top for ventilation.

In the summer it is possible to allow your cavies out onto a grassed area in a suitable fenced area. The most suitable way to do this is to use a type of hutch known as a Morant. It was invented by Major Morant towards the end of the 19th Century mainly to be used by Rabbits and Poultry, but it is very useful for guinea pigs. It is a hutch which allows the animals it contains to graze directly from a lawn or grassy patch. It consists basically of a triangular arc, two thirds of which is covered with wire netting, the remaining third being covered by a wooden house. The whole of the floor area is also covered with wire netting to stop the animals from digging their way out; (although this is very rare in guinea pigs) yet still allowing them to graze from the grass upon which the hutch is resting. To prevent

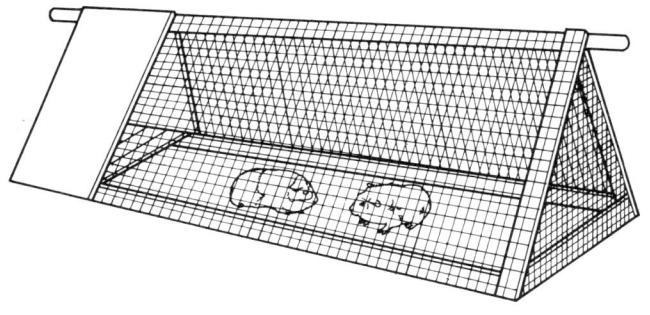

A Morant hutch

fouling of any particular area the hutch should be moved daily to a new patch. A good size Morant is about 300 cms in length and 80 cms high. The house part should take up about 100 cms of the length and should be covered with tongue and groove boarding. Inside the house a raised shelf should be fitted to enable the animals to sleep on a dry surface should they wish. This type of hutch is meant to be easily transported and therefore should not be made too heavy. Naturally this type of hutch is meant only for small groups of animals for short periods and only during fine weather, never in the winter.

Bedding and Litter

Bedding serves two purposes. It gives warmth and it soaks up urine and thereby keeps the guinea pigs clean. Some people start with a layer of newspaper then a top layer of wood shavings or sawdust. I personally do not like the use of newspaper as some guinea pigs will eat it and can easily be poisoned by the newsprint; instead I use wood shavings to a depth of about 10 cm/2 inches. In addition to this you should provide a good handful of hay per guinea pig. The guinea pig will eat the hay so it must be kept topped up.

Cleaning out

You should clean out your hutches once a week, unless the weather is very cold. In this situation, providing the bedding is not wet on top, it can be covered with a fresh layer of shavings and hay.

3 Feeding Your Guinea Pig

When you buy your guinea put it is a wise precaution to ask the seller what he has been feeding it on. Then if you wish to change the diet you may do so gradually and not upset the digestion of the individual.

The essential items of a quinea pig's diet are:

1. Hay and Water
2. Cereals in some form
3. Green foods and roots
4. Occasional supplements

These are not in any particular order, but all are essential and none should be left out.

Water

Water is best provided in bottles sold in the pet shops for this purpose. The best are those with a stainless steel tube, as the cavy will then be unable to chew through them.

Hay

As with water, hay should be given freely, giving more when it has been either eaten or soiled. Without hay guinea pigs cannot digest what they have eaten.

Guinea pigs prefer soft meadow hay to the coarser type, but this may be used if the softer hay is not

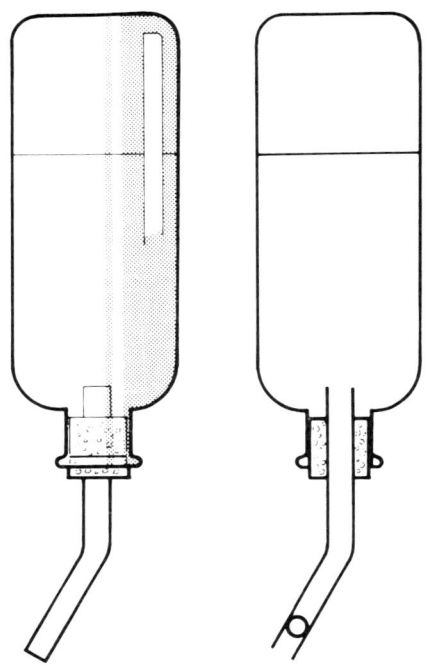

Two different types of drinking bottle

available. The smell alone will tell you if the hay is fresh it should not smell of mould nor should it be dusty or show signs of mildew. Apart from food, hay also provides a better source of warmth as bedding than anything else.

Straw should not be used as the sharp ends can easily damage the large eyes of guinea pigs as they burrow into it.

Cereals

The major proportion of guinea pig fanciers give a basic diet of some form of seed and cereal mixture. Usually

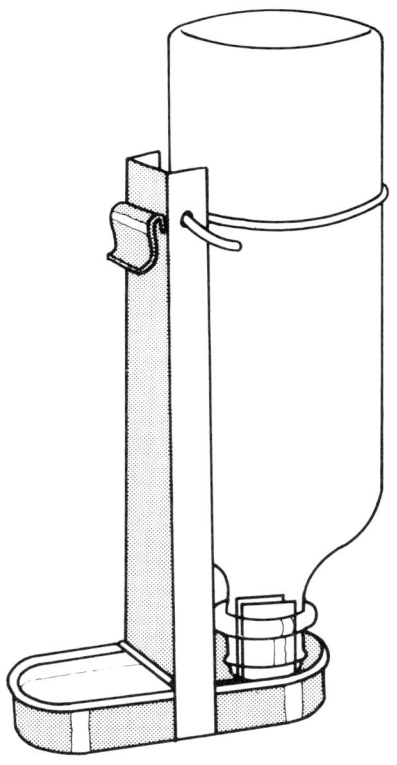

A bottle drinker which takes ordinary lemonade bottles

this contains crushed oats, wheat, barley, some form of maize, rabbit pellets and puppy biscuits. I use a goat mixture which I have found my animals enjoy more than any other mix I have as yet come across. This particular mix contains all the above ingredients with the addition of dried flaked vegetables, and molassine meal. With this mix I find much less waste than with other.

Green Foods and Vegetables

Various green foods and vegetables may be fed to guinea pigs, although a few do need to be fed with a little thought. Therefore I have listed below a selection of the most commonly available foods and the problems or lack of them.

Lettuce

Although lettuce is the most popular of all green foods for people to feed to rodents, not just guinea pigs, it can be very dangerous if fed in excess as it can cause a serious liver complaint. Lettuce is a useful food, but in small amounts only.

Cabbage

This to can be dangerous if over fed, in any one meal. The outer leaves are the most beneficial, the inner having little food value in comparison, particularly in the white varieties.

Cauliflower

Without a doubt one of the best of all the cultivated vegetable greenstuffs. It has a less dramatic effect on the system than others, the leaves and stalks that are usually discarded by the cooks are the best food value and guinea pigs always seem to enjoy them.

Chicory

Another very useful greenstuff, but it is rather difficult to obtain in some areas of the country and therefore maybe rather expensive. It is not only good in food value but is also a rather valuable tonic.

Spinach

Again a valuable tonic, it is good and rich in both vitamins and minerals, however it is vey strong tasting and some guinea pigs take a dislike to it for this reason.

Sprouts

Brussels sprouts and Sprout Tops are commonly fed, but again they are not particularly suitable in large amounts. If fed in excess they can cause a wide variety of bladder complaints.

Kale

A much overlooked vegetable that can be provided as green food. All the plant, apart from that below soil level, can be fed so there is no waste. In appearance it is very similar to cabbage. The curly variety is the most popular.

Parsley

This is a perennial herb rather than a vegetable, but it will provide green food all year around, year after year. However you may find that as with spinach some guinea pigs will not like the taste of it.

Various root vegetables may also be given including: carrot, the most popular both with fanciers and guinea pigs; beetroot (avoid this if you have white show stock as it may stain the fur); swede and turnip.

Guinea pigs also enjoy a number of other fuit and vegetables, for example: pears apples, celery, peas, beans and many more.

Flowers and Weeds

Flowers

The flowers of your garden also produce an amazing variety of foods for guinea pigs. You can feed quite a large variety of flowers but always avoid the flowers and leaves of bulbs, as these are usually poisonous to livestock.

Among the more common flowers that may be fed to guinea pigs are: marigolds; nasturtiums, phlox, asters wallflowers, salvias, sweet peas, cornflowers and alyssum.

Weeds

By far the easiest weed to obtain for your stock is grass. Guinea pigs just adore it.

Many other weeds or wild flowers maybe fed to your stock, however they are not always that easy to recognise and a few are highly dangerous, for example the buttercup is very dangerous when fresh. It is impossible for me to list all those plants that are suitable here as there are so many, but the following short list gives a few of the most common. If you do not know what a plant looks like, do check with a plant identification guide and do not pick plants if you are not sure what they are:

Burnet	Dock	Plaintain
Cow Parsley	Groundsel	Shepherds Purse
Coltsfoot	Hedge Parsley	Sow Thistle
Chickweed	Knot Grass	Trefoil
Crosswort	Mallow	Vetch
Dandelion	Nipplewort	Watercress
Dock	Yarrow	

It is essential that you know what you are feeding to your stock as a large number of plants are dangerous to guinea pigs. Also never take a whole plant as this is now illegal, and make sure that you are not collecting from an area that has been sprayed with chemicals or visited by animals. Remember, if in doubt leave it out.

Supplements

Guinea pigs, along with primates are unable to create their own Vitamin C and therefore require it in their diet. In summer, if they are allowed plenty of green foods, they should get enough vitamin C, but in the winter it is best to give some form of vitamin supplement. this may be given in the form of a ascorbic acid tablet dropped into the drinking water daily or Rosehip syrup or baby orange juice given in the water or on the food.

You cannot overdose this vitamin as it is water soluble and any excess will be excreted in the urine of the guinea pig. You can however overdose if you give it in the form of Cod Liver Oil. As it is an oil, it is stored in the body and may cause paralysis, should you wish to give some form of oil vitamin supplement please ensure that it is a polyunsaturated oil such as *Vitapet* or something similar.

When to feed

Give the guinea pig two separate meals. The dry cereal in the morning along with hay, and the vegetables in the evening, again with the addition of hay. Grass etc maybe given at any time, do not store grass as it will start to heat up and will then be unsuitable to be fed to your cavies.

Feeding dishes can be a bit of a problem but they are necessary. Cavies often throw them around their hutches or even use them as toilets. Therefore feeding dishes should be too heavy to throw, or should be the half moon shaped type and fixed to the wire netting of the door of the hutch.

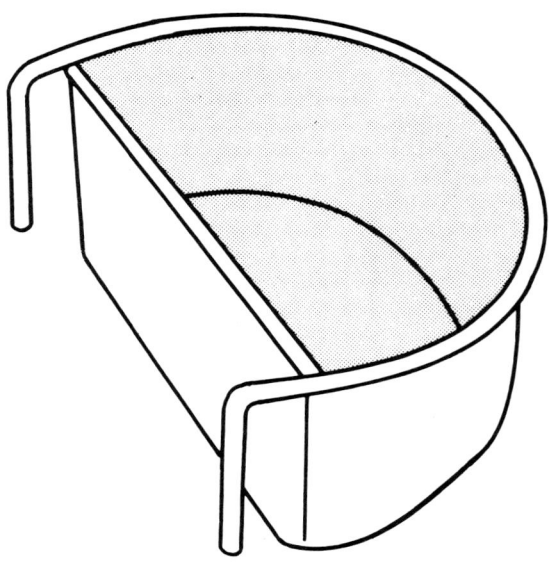

Half moon food hopper

4 **Handling and Sexing**

The correct way to pick up your guinea pig is to place one hand across the shoulders of the animal with the thumb behind the front leg on one side. The fingers then fall naturally into place over the shoulders and across the back of the animal and are well forward, curling just underneath the rib cage. The grip must be firm but not squeezing. Place the other hand under the individual's rump, to give support for the remainder of the lifting operation. Extra care should be taken when a pregnant guinea pig is being lifted.

Sexing guinea pigs is fairly easy at any age, though it is helpful if someone with experience shows you at least once. After lifting the animal, turn it onto its back. With its weight supported by the palm of the hand put gentle pressure on either side of the genitalia. Moving the finger and thumb slightly apart will extrude the penis of the boar (male) cavy quite easily, sows (females) of course, have no such extrusion.

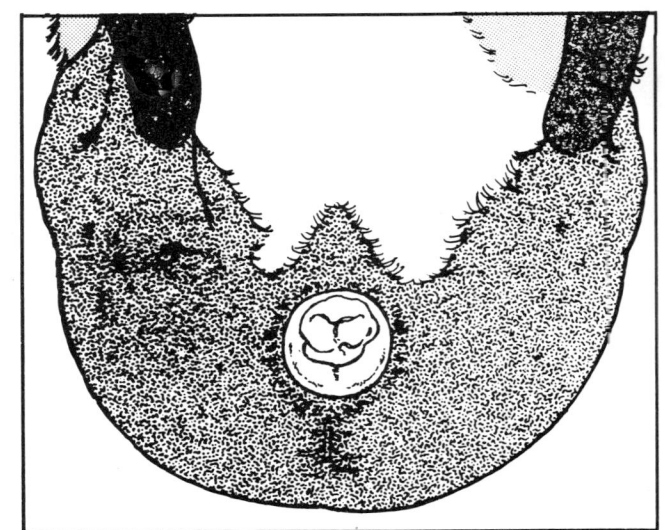

Male

Female

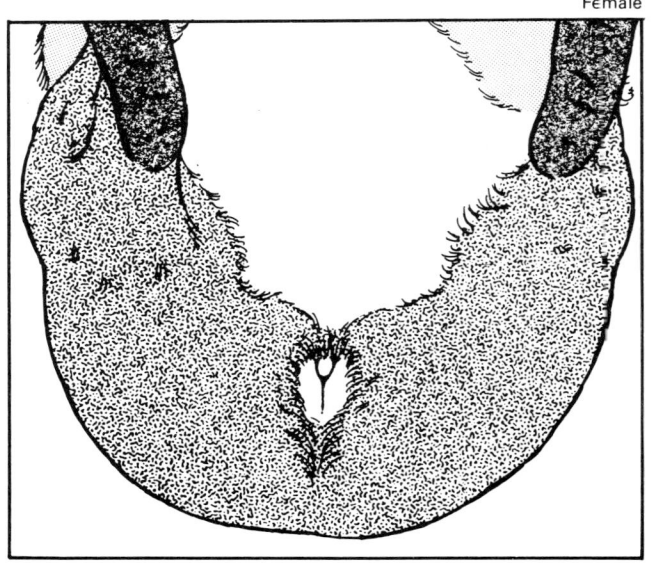

5   Health

On the whole if guinea pigs are well fed and housed they have very few health problems. However even the best kept guinea pig studs suffer from the occasional illness or accident. In years gone by the general idea seemed to be (and if you talk) to some guinea pig fanciers still is) an ill guinea pig is a dead guinea pig. However as more guinea pigs are kept, more is learned about them and their illnesses, which in turn means more are being successfully treated. However a guinea pig that is ill will often just give up and die. Likewise some may die before you are even aware that there is anything wrong with them.

Fighting Injuries

Usually an adult boar will live quite happily with an immature boar. But it is rare indeed for two adult boars to live together successfully, and should two adult boars be placed together you are likely to have a very serious fight on your hands. On occasions sows may also fight, particularly when they are establishing hutch supremacy, but this is usually not serious, very rarely you may come across a particularly disagreeable sow, who makes life in her group a misery. She is best removed and placed either with a boar or retained on her own.

Teeth

Sometimes a guinea pig will break its front teeth in a fall or from chewing the wire of its hutch. They will easily grow again quite quickly but until they do, if the break is uneven, they should be trimmed to an even length with nail clippers.

Cutting teeth is not painful for a guinea pig, but he may not like the idea and may wriggle. Get someone to hold the guinea pig for you while you clip the teeth, be careful you do not cut the tongue. If you are a bit worried about doing this yourself you can always ask at one of the shows for someone to show you how to do it or take the animal to a vet.

Nails

The nails of some guinea pigs never need cutting at all, whilst others require frequent trimming, particularly on the front feet where on occasions if you are not careful they may grow right round and go into or under the foot.

In a light coloured variety it is easy to see how far to cut the claw as the pink quick is clearly visible, but on darker varieties it is more difficult, so trim off only a little at a time until the nail looks a more comfortable length. If you should happen to cut too far and the nail bleeds, dip the claw in unperfumed talcum powder, this will stop the bleeding.

Abcesses

These are occasionally caused by knocks or fights or thistles and thorns in the hay. A fairly hard lump will be felt usually on the throat or neck. It is best to leave this alone, if it is an abcess it will slowly grow, often to an

The correct way to clip the claws

Claw clippers

enormous size and will become softer when it is getting ready to burst. The individual should be removed to a pen on its own, because if the abcess does burst the other guinea pigs may become infected by licking the wound. When it bursts a lot of pus will come out. Wipe this gently away and wash with either warm salt water or a mild antiseptic solution daily until the wound is healed.

Eye Injuries

It often happens, particularly with young stock that a stalk of hay will poke the guinea pig in the eye, causing the eye to become opaque. Usually this will clear in quite a short space of time. A small amount of golden eye ointment will help. Always ensure that no small piece of stalk or grain husk is still in the eye.

Skin Complaints

The guinea pig seems to be particularly prone to various skin troubles. One of the commonest being called by all types of names from *Sellnick* to *Rat Mange*. It is caused by a small mite which burrows under the skin surface. The first signs are tiny raised spots on the skin which itself becomes scurfy and the hair begins to fall out. These areas itch and so the guinea pig scratches. If your animals starts losing small patches of hair or has scratch marks on its coat; this is probably the cause. There are several different treatments, but I have found the most effective is to wash the guinea pig in warm water using *Tetmosol* soap, a human skin care product available from most good chemists. Repeat the bath twice more at 14 day intervals.

A number of fanciers wash their guinea pigs at regular

intervals to prevent this. It is uncertain from where this mite comes but it is most likely found in hay.

Post Natal Sores

After giving birth sows often develop a sore on their back. This is often due to a mineral protein deficiency. To avoid this, in late pregnancy, give sows about a quarter of a teaspoon of soya flour mixed with a little milk stirred into their food and sprinkle on wheat germ and mineral salts.

Also after they have littered, you will find sows with raw areas on the rump and under the belly. This is not a vitamin problem, it is caused by the sow pulling the hair out when she is cleaning herself up after the birth. It is probable that she had a long or difficult labour and by the time she got around to cleaning herself, the blood had dried on her coat and she had problems removing it. If you notice in time, then it should be possible to sponge her clean and dab her dry. The area can be rubbed with some mild oil to grease the skin and promote new hair growth.

Pregnancy Toxaemia

This usually occurs in sows in late pregnancy, but on occasions it may occur in other stock. An overweight sow, in late pregnancy, is extremely close to physiological breakdown and any extra stress can bring on Toxaemia. In tests it was found that all that was necessary to induce toxaemia was to withhold green foods. When the guinea pig is under stress, the liver overacts and vast quantities of stored fat enter the blood stream at poison levels. The blood becomes too acid; the kidneys work overtime trying to clear it and the guinea pig dies of kidney failure. The guinea pig usually appears to have muscle spasms and goes into a coma and dies. Unfortunately little can be done at this stage, but if you make sure your guinea pigs are fit but not fat before breeding you may never encounter this complaint.

Impacted Rectum

As guinea pigs grow old, especially boars, you may find they have a lump of faecal matter blocked in the rectum. The only thing you can do is to squeeze it out gently with a soft tissue wad and clean the area with warm olive oil. It is a most unpleasant task with a smell to match, but in old animals it is a problem that may well occur and it may be necessary to clean it out weekly.

A Word of Warning

When giving any medicines to guinea pigs, please be careful as not all medicines suit them. Penicillin causes anaphylactic shock and usually kills guinea pigs, although it can safely be given to a mouse or a hamster.

6 **Breeding Your Guinea Pig**

American Rex female with three day old young

Starting Breeding

You could actually start breeding when your sow is six weeks old. However, it is much better for the health of the sow if you wait until she is at least 20 weeks of age, but you don't want to leave it too long after this. The reason for this needs to be explained; as a general rule with most animals it is inadvisable to breed from young females who may have reached puberty but who are too immature in behaviour to deal with their own young competently. The same applies if they are physically immature and the pelvis has not reached an adequate size to prevent pain and difficulty during the actual birth (dystocia). The case of the guinea pig is rather different however, because there is a greater risk of dystocia if the guinea pig does not have her first litter while she is still young. Once fully mature, the pelvic bones fuse, leaving her with a rigid, perhaps undersized pelvis and this may cause difficult births. It is for this reason that a first litter should be produced before a sow is one year old. The litter will then be born before the two halves of the pelvis fuse together. Subsequent births should be trouble free.

Do not breed stock that is in any way unhealthy or sows that are overweight. You can run more than one sow with a boar, up to four or even five providing you have a large enough run or hutch. A sow will come into season once every two weeks and this lasts a few hours. On rare occasions a sow will not like a particular boar and will not mate with him. In this case, you will have to put her with a different boar. Sows are usually left with a boar for several weeks so it is not always possible to tell exactly when they have mated. The usual length of pregnancy or gestation is 65 – 72 days; therefore if you count 65 days from the day they were put together, that is the earliest date a litter may be expected.

Always be gentle handling a pregnant or 'in pig' sow. To lift them from their hutch, use both hands and use your fingers to give some support to the belly. As they get nearer to their time to litter you will be quite amazed at how large your sow will become; it may even get to the stage where you begin to think that she is going to burst. Don't worry, this large size is quite common because guinea pigs are born extremely well developed. About 48 hours before birth you can feel that the pelvic bones are opening, ready for the birth. Litters can number anything from one to six or more, although three appears to be the most common. Sows only have two nipples to feed their young, but they usually manage to raise four or five quite well.

If the sow is still in with the boar when she litters, he will not harm the young deliberately, but the sow comes into season again an hour or so after the birth and he will try to mate her, therefore the babies may be injured in the scuffle of the mating. This is not really fair on the sow as it greatly adds to the strain on her not only feeding a litter but also carrying another as well.

If two sows 'in pig' share a hutch, and one of them litters, this may, (although it is quite rare) excite the other so much that she will abort her litter. Therefore it is usually best to remove a sow that is due to litter into a hutch on her own a few days before she is actually due to give birth. She may always be returned to her old hutch along with her litter a week or so after their birth.

Difficult Births

99.9% of all guinea pig births are perfectly normal, usually the first thing you know of it is when you go to their hutch to give them their meal and you find you have more guinea pigs than the last time you looked. However, there is the rare occasion when your sow will have problems. One of the commonest cause is large litters. Unfortunately there is no way that you can prevent this.

What must you do if one of your animals appears to be in difficulties? If the babies head is protruding, you can grip it gently with a clean cloth and gently ease the baby out. Be careful not to pull too hard or you may cause prolapse of the females uterus. If the baby's head has not appeared and the mother is in obvious difficulties, you can insert your little finger and hook your finger nail or to the baby's teeth and then gently ease it out. If it's a breech birth you maybe able to make it move to the correct position by gently massaging the abdomen of the sow in a circular movement. If you are at all nervous about doing any of this, then take your sow to your vet at once.

Large Litters

Large litters may be split up and fostered quite easily onto sows that only have one or two young of their own. Usually this is most successfully done when the babies are only a few days old. It is much more difficult if there is an age gap of more than a few days between the two litters as the older babies will tend to push the younger ones aside.

To introduce the litters rub some damp sawdust from the foster mother's hutch onto the baby. If the mother starts to fuss and lick it then she will accept the baby. However, if she will not accept it she will keep pushing it away, grind her teeth, and may even bite the baby, although sows do not usually hurt them. In such cases the baby will have to be returned to its original mother who will not mind the smell of the other sow's hutch.

Hand Rearing

If the babies do not appear to be getting enough food, or if the mother should die, you can either supplement their milk intake or hand rear the litter. Use an eye dropper, and feed a milk powder mixed with a little warm water and glucose solution. At first you should feed them every two hours at least for the first day or so, ideally this should be through the night as well, but one feed at night is usually enough. They soon become adept at sucking at the dropper, but do not squeeze the milk into their mouths or they will choke, let them take it at their own pace, about one eye dropper full each at first and increase it to whatever they will take. In addition to this it is always best to put a mixture of bran together with a little brown bread soaked in milk in a shallow dish so that they can get accustomed to helping themselves. Once they do this, keep the dish clean and freshly filled each day and stop dropper feeding except for any small individuals. You will probably have to clean up the baby's mouth as its mother would. They should in addition to their milk/bran mixture have exactly the same food as the adult guinea pigs but if you are giving them root vegetables it is advisable to mince or grate these for a few days.

When to have Litters

Do not allow your sow to have more than three litters in any one year, and do not allow her to become fat when she is not with a boar as this will also cause problems.

Guinea pigs make great pets!

Most sows will stop breeding at about three years of age although some will stop before this and some will go on until they are five. The average life span is five to six years although I have known guinea pigs to live until they are seven or eight.

I rarely allow my own sows to litter between December and March. It is during this part of the winter when individual animals are at their lowest and food is beginning to deteriorate due to storage. Feeding a pregnant sow during the winter months must be given a little more thought than feeding one that isn't pregnant. She must not be allowed to become fat but at the same time must eat enough not only to provide for herself but also for her unborn babies. Give plenty of good hay, a supply of fresh vitamin C bearing foods, should be available daily as well as her normal dry food diet.

Separating the Sexes

Babies are usually fed by their mother for approximately four weeks and they should then be separated into their different sexes. Young males will tolerate each other until they are about three to four months old when they will usually start to become aggressive, chattering their teeth which is a sign of aggression. An adult boar will usually tolerate a young boar as company. If he is on his own but he will not tolerate a young boar if there are females in the hutch.

Breeding Records

If you are keeping and breeding guinea pigs with showing as your ultimate aim, detailed records should be maintained for each animal. It is most important that a breeder can see at a glance which stock has been bred from which individuals, and which combination of animals produces the best results. By far the simplest way of doing this is to give each individual guinea pig a card. This card can be stored in an index box. You should record such information as the name of the animal, its parents, grandparents, colour, age, the date of all litters borne or sired by it, the size of litter and their sex and colour. Then from the information that is contained on these cards, detailed pedigrees can be formulated and should a rare variety be produced its ancestry can then be traced back and it may be therefore possible to produce another by the same means.

7 Showing Guinea Pigs

Should you decide you would like to show guinea pigs, the first thing to do is to go along to one of your local shows. Talk to the local breeders and try to decide which variety you would like to keep. If you already have a guinea pig that you believe may be worth showing, take it along with you and ask one of the fanciers whether or not it is worth showing and if so in which class.

There are a number of clubs you can join, your local one in the area, the national club or the specialist club for your chosen variety. Most local clubs put on shows which cater for all breeds available even if some are only in an Any Other Variety section.

The advantages of showing, apart from the enjoyment you will get out of it, are more obvious to the experienced breeder than the beginner. You will meet other breeders and you will demonstrate to others how good you are at keeping and breeding your particular variety. The prizes to be won even at national level are quite small, perhaps only a rosette or a small cup.

Most shows are governed by national rules and these rarely vary. Different classes are held for young and adult animals, boars and sows, varieties etc. Class winners are entered in best of breed, best sow, best boar and best in show. Special care is needed in grooming to ensure that your guinea pig is seen at its very best.